7.60

CLAUDIO MON

TEN M

D0851060

Edited by Denis Stevens

DATE DUE

782.4

M781

23569

920

OXFORD UNIVERSITY PRESS

Music Department, 44 Conduit Street, London WIR ODE

PREFACE

To bar or not to bar, that is the question. Ever since musical scholars began their self-appointed and apparently ceaseless task of making the repertoire of earlier times available in brand-new editions, discussions ranging from the argumentative to the dialectical have continued to enliven the musicological scene and to generate — by theory out of practice — countless novel methods of transcription. These can be found and studied in the serried ranks of scholarly volumes on the one hand, while on the other we have a more humble counterpart, ranging from the practical performing edition to the edition that is practically unperformable. And it is axiomatic that vocal and choral music stands to lose or gain more than any other genre, because of the additional complexities introduced by prose or poetry.

The historical viewpoint is encouragingly clear. In those early centuries when polyphony was cradled and nourished, skilled singers could read with equal ease from single voice-parts or from conductus notation, this latter being a kind of quasi-score in which the notes belonging to a chord were arranged vertically, even though they were not precisely aligned. Examples of both methods may be seen in *The Old Hall Manuscript*, III (London, 1938) between pages xxiv and xxv, and at the frontispiece, where Chirbury's *Sanctus* contains what at first glance seem to be bar-lines, but which are actually sectional boundaries.

When music-printing appeared, the idea of the part-book won immediate favour and support, so much so that printed scores or quasi-scores rarely saw the light of day. Exceptions to this general rule were nevertheless notable: Lampadius, in his *Compendium musices* of 1537, printed the opening of a four-voice Marian antiphon by Philippe Verdelot, in open score with regular bar-lines; in 1577 all of Rore's four-part madrigals were published in score (also with bar-lines) for the benefit of keyboard players and students of composition; and in 1613 Simone Molinaro issued Gesualdo's madrigals in open score with bar-lines placed between units of one, two, or three semibreves according to the phrasing and implied tempo of the music.

Manuscript scores diligently constructed by individual and often anonymous enthusiasts, inspired no doubt by the dictum that the whole is worth more than the sum of its parts, exist in fair abundance throughout the sixteenth and seventeenth centuries, as Edward Lowinsky has demonstrated in his article 'Early Scores in Manuscript' (*Journal of the American Musicological Society*, XIII, 1960, 126-173). These are invariably characterized by a ruthless, regular kind of barring that usually extends from top to bottom of the score, nonchalantly dissecting not only the music but the text in much the same way as a grid would appear to chop into squares a reproduction of a famous painting. Such devices certainly make analysis and copying easier than they might otherwise prove to be, but they also have the disadvantage of interfering with the flow of pen or brush.

Although the current practice of making printed part-books available once again in the form of facsimiles has already tempted specialized groups into using them for performance, it is highly unlikely that this movement will spread very far. A facsimile tends to be expensive; a part-book is very hard to rehearse from; and even if these factors (together with unfamiliar notational features and textual problems) can be satisfactorily overcome, there is no guarantee whatsoever that any resulting performance will be noticeably superior as regards accuracy of ensemble, or vitality and sensitivity of interpretation. These qualities are entirely dependent upon the musicians and the director; and even though the singers can make do with parts, the director needs a score.

Generally speaking, the vocal score has proved to be the most suitable among modern printed media for motets, madrigals and the like. It can easily dispense with that anachronistic space-waster, the piano accompaniment for rehearsal, because any musician cast for that role can just as readily provide the requisite support by playing from the familiar treble and bass lines of the score. It can likewise banish irrevocably an even worse invention, the 'reduction for instrumental accompaniment', whose advocates erroneously assume that all madrigals should be performed either as accompanied solos or with the several voice-parts doubled by instruments.

Although in certain circumstances a modest measure of instrumental participation may not be unwelcome, it should be borne in mind that composers were quite often concerned about vocal lines maintaining their independence and purity. In the preface to his *First Book of Madrigals à 5*, published at Venice in 1620 and dedicated to the Duke of Bracciano, Cesare Zoilo states that he 'composed these madrigals with the intention of having them sung by five voices only, without any instrumental accompaniment whatsoever, and he begs and prays that they may be so sung'. The only exception, according to Zoilo, is the continuo part; but this does not concern us in the performance of the Monteverdi madrigals here transcribed.

They are presented in open score, as is customary, yet they introduce a new kind of transcription which has hitherto been used only in manuscript editions from which the Accademia Monteverdiana has performed or recorded. The primary aim is to allow the music and text to proceed in a natural and untrammelled way, which it cannot and does not do in earlier types of edition. The opening bars of *Crudel, perchè mi fuggi* appear opposite in four different guises in order to facilitate comparison, beginning with the traditional Regular barring, which cuts up text as well as music, besides obscuring hemiolas and inducing faulty stress (downbeat on the weak syllables '-gi' and '-o'). Mensurstrich frees the music more — except where the alto goes below the staff — but boxes in the text. Bizarre barring, which has been used at various times by Leichtentritt, Fellowes, Gombosi and others, attempts to bring the stressed syllables immediately after the bar-line (where singers tend to stress), but the confusing and out-of-phase visual effect quickly undermines this apparent advantage. In the Accademia barring, a natural and effortless alternation of 2-beat and 3-beat units clarifies the hemiolas, brings the stressed syllables together on strong beats, and permits both text and music to flow as they deserve: 'Cru_del_, per_chè_ mi _fuggi_, S'hai de la _mor_te _mia_ _tan_to de_si_o'.

1. Regular barring

2. Mensurstrich

3. Bizarre barring

4. Accademia barring

The point of departure for Accademia barring is the 1613 edition of Gesualdo's madrigals, where the alternation of duple and triple groupings is clearly shown by the placement of bar-lines. This can easily be studied from the partial facsimiles in Wilhelm Weismann's edition (Ugrino Verlag, Hamburg). An earlier though comparable attempt to induce an easy flow between groups of three, four and six beats may be found in Cavalieri's *Rappresentatione di anima, e di corpo*, notably in the homophonic choruses (Rome, 1600; Gregg Press reprint, 1967). Yet the early publishers of Cavalieri and Gesualdo were not completely aware of the possibilities they had begun to open up, and few have subsequently drawn attention to the matter. The best discussion in recent years is that of Glenn Watkins in his *Gesualdo* (London, 1973), 45, 177.

The duple-triple flow was sensed, nevertheless, by certain scholars engaged in the investigation of Medieval and Renaissance repertoire and its notational problems. H. B. Briggs, founder of the Plainsong and Medieval Music Society, points out in his preface to *The Musical Notation of the Middle Ages* (London, 1890), that in music prior to the early sixteenth century, the mensural interpretation of a melody was probably dependent on the text to which it was sung, varying continually from duple to triple measure. Although this principle has not so far been applied to Italian music, E. H. Fellowes made some use of it, as did the editors of *Tudor Church Music*, the first volume of which (Oxford University Press, 1923), contains an anonymous preface where the following statement may be found:

'In this edition the barring is irregular, with the object of emphasizing the rhythmic structure more strongly than would be possible with conventional regular barring. Time-signatures, having only arithmetical significance, allow of the alternation of long or short sections of duple or triple rhythm, and of their indication by means of bar-lines, and the same principle of alternation is indicated in the unbarred MSS. by black notation and the extra-mensural use of the dot. Where the music is homophonic or semi-homophonic irregular barring is clearly called for.'

It so happens that much of the music composed in the style which Monteverdi christened *seconda prattica* exploits chordal passages notable for their audibility of text and clarity of declamation. The text was 'mistress of the harmony' in the sense that it dictated not only the relative length of each chord, but also the grouping of successive chords in blocks of two, three, or more, depending on the metre or meaning of the poem. To be sure, other elements of the second practice were usually present: the perfection of melody, which (like the text) took frequent precedence over harmony, and the innovative treatment of dissonances, of which there are countless examples in the music of Rore, de Wert, Luzzaschi, Nenna, Gesualdo, Peri, Fontanelli, Pallavicino, and others. But the main feature — power of declamation — was immediately taken over as a *sine qua non* in the rapidly developing music-drama of the late Renaissance, where the choruses had to be sung 'most simply and in such a way that they seem to differ only a little from ordinary speech' — to quote from Angelo Ingegneri's treatise on theatre production, as translated by Carol MacClintock.

Although every madrigal in the present anthology contains some passages in homophonic style, by far the most numerous occur in the wonderfully expressive setting of *Ch'io t'ami,* from Act III Scene 3 of Guarini's *Il Pastor Fido*. The three cleverly linked episodes from Mirtillo's lengthy castigation of the reluctant Amarilli provide remarkable and memorable examples of a musically sensitive attitude towards natural speech-rhythms. Questions and answers, prayers and reproaches, rhetorical figures and word-play, all are reflected and intensified by the relentless rhythms that rise effortlessly to a climax and then fall as gently to a finely-chiselled cadence. But the full impact of the work can only be felt and understood when strategically-placed bar-lines prompt performers to give the necessary weight to the right syllables.

❀   ❀   ❀

The following examples show, by means of comparison, the considerable advantages of Accademia barring over the conventional kind. Example 1(b), from *Filli cara e amata* , demonstrates how a simple shift of the bar-line removes unwanted ties, replacing them with dotted notes or whole notes (as the case may be) which reflect accurately the composer's original notation. The same shift also takes care of the verbal accentuation, avoiding the danger of false stresses on weak syllables: ingrata, nieghi, prieghi.

Example 1

At the beginning of *Dolcemente dormiva la mia Clori*, the hemiola rhythm that cannot fail to be obscured by conventional barring stands clearly revealed when matters are arranged as in Example 2(b):

Example 2

Notwithstanding the editorial penchant for barring in units of two minims, musical phrase-lengths in madrigals of the *seconda prattica* often make use of a three-minim unit, suggested perhaps by the metre of the poem, as in Example 3 which sets forth a typical passage from *Quell' augellin che canta:*

Example 3

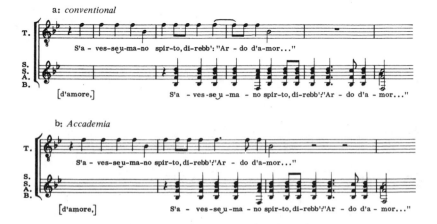

The visible and audible effect of the responsorial passage above can easily be recaptured in a slightly more complex situation such as the opening of *Oimè il bel viso*, provided that bar-lines are placed in a manner calculated to enhance Monteverdi's sensitive treatment of Petrarch's verse. Example 4 shows how the correspondence between verbal and musical phrases moves from near darkness to clear light as soon as macrorhythmic principles are adopted.

Example 4

a: *conventional*

b: *Accademia*

Long experience has proved that singers working at a madrigal with regular barring tend to suffer from a kind of metrical claustrophobia. They know and feel that the inspiration of both poet and composer languishes behind bars, through which the monotonous and ineffectual sawing of a tactus beat is powerless to cut. No matter how much they rehearse, the real subtleties always seem to elude them, but it is neither their fault nor the fault of their director. Given an edition in which Accademia barring releases the proper flow of music and verse, the performers will notice an immediate improvement, and they will also be made aware of the need for occasional pauses as well as for a measure of flexibility in tempo.

The score of Cavalieri's *Rappresentatione* is full of .S˙ signs, which he asks the singers to interpret as pauses, so that they can 'take a breath and give a little time to the execution of some motive or other'. The twofold object of this exercise is just as worthy of attention today as it was in 1600, for musicians as well as musical phrases deserve breathing-space and the resulting leeway provides time for the sense to sink in, not to mention the avoidance of a strictly mechanical interpretation of the prevailing metre.

That such an approach is also applicable to the music of Monteverdi and his contemporaries may be gathered from a letter sent by Aquilino Coppini to Hendrik van der Putten of Louvain in July 1609. This letter, accompanying three sets of Coppini's spiritualized madrigal collections — *Musica tolta da i Madrigali di Claudio Monteverde , et d'altri autori* — explains that the works of the Cremonese master 'require longer pauses, and (as it were) the beating of time between the singing; resting occasionally, allowing retardation, and at times even pressing on'. Since Coppini was a close friend and admirer of Monteverdi, his advice would almost certainly have been based on what he heard and observed at performances directed by the composer himself, and it follows that those who wish to reproduce the spirit of those performances today ought to allow their singers adequate breathing-space and exhort them to cultivate the gentle art of rubato, remembering that *ars est celare artem.*

To these recommendations of 1600 and 1609, a further one is added from 1615, when the second edition (with augmented contents and revised preface) of Frescobaldi's first book of *Toccate e Partite* came off the press of Nicolò Borboni in Rome. The player is advised to avoid strict time, just as he would when performing modern madrigals — 'which, however difficult, become fluent and manageable when the beat is now slow, now fast, and even sometimes held or sustained in the air in keeping with the emotional content of the music and the meaning of its text'. Frescobaldi, like Coppini, advocates the variation of tempi and close attention to pauses, when the beat is 'sustained in the air'.

The fourth and last piece of advice to performers comes from the pen of Monteverdi. It appears in his *Madrigali Guerrieri et Amorosi* (1638), as a brief note appended to the chaconne best known under the title of *Lamento della Ninfa*, although the actual plaint is framed by an introduction and coda for two tenors and bass. The composer tells us that the director should beat time in these two sections, but not in the Lament, which 'should be sung at a tempo dictated by the emotions, not by the beat'. Significantly, this Lament is a miniature madrigal for four voices, and even though the soprano dominates the scene and the vocal ensemble is supported by continuo instruments, there is a close analogy between the spirit of this work and the earlier ones presented here.

In order to assist modern performers, I have added pauses at appropriate points, in the form of rests enclosed in square brackets; material printed small and cautionary accidentals in brackets are editorial. By collating the available early editions of these madrigals, I have established a text which — now shorn of obvious errors and omissions — aims to convey the essence of Monteverdi's musical thought. Yet the marriage of music and poetry is not without its own peculiar problems, one of which concerns the correct underlaying of text. A case in point is the opening of *Zefiro torna,* of which Example 5 shows a comparison between the accepted but wrongly accented version, and the present revision.

Example 5

Another closely-related problem is when to change from one vowel to the next in a word such as 'mio', which is often placed below one note. In those instances that might cause confusion, I have divided the one note into two, either equal or unequal depending on the context, so that the point of change can be made smoothly and with regard to the matter of relative stress. Orthography has generally been modernized, since there is little point in printing 'Hor' for 'Or' when the aspirate is unpronounced, to give but one example. As an aid to good ensemble and clarity of texture, certain chords have been adjusted in length. Dynamics have been left to the discretion of conductors, who will doubtless find the necessary hints in the poetry, here newly translated for their benefit.

For advice and assistance in preparing this edition, I should like to express my warmest thanks to the musicians of the Accademia Monteverdiana, and to Edward Hain de Lara, Alec Harman and Glenn Watkins.

Santa Barbara, California, 1977   *Denis Stevens*

N. B. — Translations by the Editor are meant neither for singing nor for reproduction. The word-order has been arranged to follow that of the Italian text as far as possible, in order to assist the reader in understanding the emotional content of individual words and phrases.

TEN MADRIGALS

Edited by
Denis Stevens

CLAUDIO MONTEVERDI
(1567 - 1643)

1. FILLI CARA E AMATA

Source: Madrigals, Book I, 1587 (Venice, Angelo Gardano)

Count Marco Verità, dedicatee of these youthful compositions likened to the flowers of spring by the modest 20-year-old Monteverdi, was not a nobleman of Cremona, as is generally supposed. He lived in the old Roman city of Verona when it was part of the Venetian *terra ferma*, and together with his brother Count Gasparo did much to encourage music and poetry, especially in the famous Accademia Filarmonica where Marc' Antonio Ingegneri was director of music. Ingegneri, who is acknowledged as Monteverdi's teacher on the title-page of these madrigals, undoubtedly assisted his brilliant young pupil by providing him with letters of introduction to Verità, and it is quite probable that Monteverdi spent some time in Verona in 1585 or 1586. The affectionate tone of the dedication, and the grateful acknowledgment of favours received, do seem to express a vague desire for future employment there, but after a year or so Monteverdi turned his thoughts towards Mantua. The music-loving count was the dedicatee of several other volumes, among them madrigals by the Veronese composers Fonghetto and Bozi, and he also appears as one of the characters in Pietro Ponzio's *Dialogo della Musica* (1595).

Performance: Do not underplay the sensuousness of the opening paragraph, with its concern for the 'bella bocca' and for intimate, close-knit texture. The pause in bar 12 can be lengthened if desired, and 'Ahi' lightly accented to point up Phyllis's taciturn mood. From 19 to 21 the tenors should tune and balance carefully, as at the corresponding point in the repeat, which sounds very effective when treated as an echo.

Filli cara e amata,	Dear, beloved Phyllis,
Dimmi, per cortesia,	Prithee, tell me,
Questa tua bella bocca, non è mia?	This lovely mouth of yours — is it not mine?
Ahi, non rispondi, ingrata,	Ah, you do not answer, ungrateful one,
E col silenzio nieghi	And silent you refuse
D'ascoltar i miei prieghi.	To listen to my prayers.
Piacciati almen, se taci,	Be so kind, at least, if you must remain silent,
D'usar in vece di risposta i baci.	To use, instead of words, kisses.

Alberto Parma

translated by D. S.

Printed in Great Britain

OXFORD UNIVERSITY PRESS, MUSIC DEPARTMENT, 44 CONDUIT STREET, LONDON W1R 0DE

2. CRUDEL, PERCHÈ MI FUGGI

Source: Madrigals, Book II, 1590 (Venice, Angelo Gardano)

Although the dedication of Book II is dated January 1,1590, from Cremona, Monteverdi had already left his native city to seek employment in Milan and may also have visited Mantua. The journey to Milan had brought him under the roof and patronage of Jacomo Ricardi, a lawyer and amateur musician who at that time held high office in both civil and ecclesiastical circles. He may be identical with an otherwise untraceable 'Jacomo Ricordi' who published a canzonetta in a Roman anthology of 1589, for Monteverdi's patron served as the Milanese agent in Rome from 1578 until 1589. Ricardi's brief encounter with the youthful virtuoso on the viola da brazzo was doubtless cordial, but it led to nothing permanent in the way of employment, and before the end of 1590 a firm choice had been made in favour of Mantua. Perhaps Tasso's sojourn in that city from July 1586 until October 1587 had something to do with Monteverdi's willingness to settle there, but in any event the fascination exerted by poet over composer was such that almost half of the texts in Book II are by Tasso. One poem, often attributed to him, is in fact by another: 'Crudel, perchè mi fuggi', which appears in the slightly different original form of 'Lasso, perchè mi fuggi' in Guarini's *Rime* (Venice, 1598), was often set with either incipit by late 16th-century madrigalists.

Performance: Clear tonal contrast is called for in order to distinguish between the opening question and the reassuring corollary; also in the repeat where the high and low ranges are reversed. Allow the paired seven-beat phrases (24-29) a sense of urgency; but hold back bars 30 to 38. From 39 to the end, concentrate on cross-accents in the text, and beware of hurrying just because the note-values become smaller. The overall impression is one of sorrow and lamentation.

Crudel, perchè mi fuggi,	Cruel, why dost thou fly me,
S'hai de la morte mia tanto desio?	If so my death so great content may win thee?
Tu sei pur il cor mio.	Thou hast my heart within me:
Credi tu per fuggire,	Dost thou think by thy flying,
Crudel, farmi morire?	Cruel, to see me dying?
Ah, non si può morir senza dolore,	Oh, none alive can die hurtless, ungrieved,
E doler non si può chi non ha core.	And grief can no man feel, of heart deprived.
Battista Guarini	N. Yonge: *Musica Transalpina II* (1597)

3. DOLCEMENTE DORMIVA LA MIA CLORI

Source: Madrigals, Book II, 1590 (Venice, Angelo Gardano)

Few poets have influenced music as profoundly as Torquato Tasso, and few composers reflected the beauty and power of his verse as did Monteverdi. The two may possibly have met each other in 1591, when Monteverdi had just come to Mantua and Tasso paid the city a final visit before his flight to Rome. Years before, when the poet had been imprisoned in Ferrara, his release had been arranged by Don Vincenzo Gonzaga, who later became Monteverdi's patron. Vincenzo brought Tasso to Mantua on July 14, 1586, and in that same year the Fourth Book of *Rime e Prose* was published in Venice. Among its contents, 'Dolcemente dormiva la mia Clori' appealed at once to Giovanni Gabrieli and to Monteverdi, and both composers published their settings in 1590, the Venetian choosing the medium of an eight-part dialogue, 'Dormiva dolcemente'. Apart from this transposition of the opening words, the texts are almost identical.

Performance: The correct tempo for the quiet opening should be taken from the phrase 'givan scherzando' which must not be rushed, since the flying cupids are not yet supersonic. 'Mirav' io' requires restraint, almost of a breathless nature, but the dialogue can be gently stressed in bars 20 to 24. 'Quando dirmi sentei' is a whisper; but 'Stolto' must make its full effect without being too loud. When the magic moment arrives ('E baciandole') the voices should aim at a *non vibrato* effect, which will heighten the warming of timbre and growth of tone as the peroration is reached. Special attention should be paid here to verbal cross-accents.

Dolcemente dormiva la mia Clori	My Chloris was sleeping sweetly,
E intorno al suo bel volto	And about her beautiful countenance
Givan scherzando i pargoletti amori.	Love's cherubs were playing.
Mirav' io, da me tolto,	I was looking at her
Con gran diletto lei,	Beside myself with delight,
Quando dirmi sentei: "Stolto, che fai?	When I heard someone say: "Idiot, what [are you doing?
Tempo perduto non s'acquista mai!"	Lost time never returns!"
Allor io mi chinai così pian piano,	Then I leaned over her, oh so quietly,
E baciandole il viso	And kissing her face
Provai quanta dolcezz' ha il paradiso.	Learned how much sweetness paradise [contains.
Torquato Tasso	translated by D. S.

22

4. VATTENE PUR, CRUDEL

Source: Madrigals, Book III, 1592 (Venice, Ricciardo Amadino)

From the madrigals based on Tasso's amorous lyrics in Book II, Monteverdi turned in Book III to more serious matters: a triptych from the twelfth canto of *Gerusalemme Liberata*, and another from the sixteenth canto. By a fascinating coincidence, Monteverdi later set earlier passages from the same cantos, but in recitative instead of polyphonic style — the *Combattimento di Tancredi e Clorinda* in 1624, and its parergon of 1626, the *Armida* which has not survived. Both stories belong to the additional material grafted so skilfully by Tasso on to the historical events of the First Crusade. 'Vattene pur, crudel' (canto XVI, verses 59, 60, 63) recaptures in music of heightened passion the tearful imprecations of Armida, the sensuous sorceress and sex-symbol, niece of the enchanter Idraote, at the very point when she loses her hold over Rinaldo d'Este. Tasso naturally related his hero to the Este family since he worked on and completed his great epic while he lived in Ferrara, and he would surely have approved of Monteverdi's setting, for he asked composers (in *La Cavaletta*, 1587) 'to leave aside all that music which, by its degeneration, has become soft and effeminate'.

Performance: The three madrigals have been transposed down a whole tone and combined into a symphonic entity. There must be a continuous flow of meaning, especially between the first two madrigals — bar 42 should have a semicolon, not a full stop as in the original partbooks. The singers should enter fully into the spirit of the miniature drama, expressing Armida's passion and fury with every ounce of vocal persuasion that they can muster. This does not mean that everything has to be loud: the dynamics are dictated by the meaning of each phrase. Bars 32-49 suggest a menacingly quiet imprecation; 50 a sudden outburst of fury; 61 a *subito piano*. At 64 a noticeable pause can be made in order to show the end of Armida's speech and the beginning of narrative, which ends at 121. Thereafter it should be clear that Armida has returned to the limelight. At first she is calm (141) but as she gives way to her despair, it builds up to tearful rage again (156).

"Vattene pur, crudel, con quella pace
  Che lasci a me, vattene iniqu' omai.
Me tost' ignudo spirt' ombra seguace
  Indivisibilmente a tergo avrai.
Nova Furia co' serp'e con la face
  Tanto t'agitero, quanto t'amai.
E s'è destin ch'esca del mar, che schivi
Li scogli e l'onde, e ch'a la pugna arrivi;

Là tra'l sangu'e le morti egro giacente
  Mi pagherai le pen' empió guerriero.
Per nom' Armida chiamerai sovente
  Negl' ultimi singulti: udir ciò spero."
Or qui mancò lo spirto a la dolente,
  Nè quest' ultimo suono espresse intero:
E cadde tramortita, e si diffuse
Di gelato sudor' e i lumi chiuse.

Poi ch'ella in sè tornò, deserto e muto,
  Quanto mirar potè, d'intorno scorse.
"Ito se n'è pur," diss', "ed ha potuto
  Me qui lasciar de la mia vita in forse?
Nè un moment' indugiò, nè un brev' aiuto
  Nel caso estrem' il traditor mi porse?
Et io pur anco l'amo, e' n questo lido
Invendicata ancor piango e m'assido?"

Tasso: *Gerusalemme Liberata*
(Canto XVI, 59, 60, 63)

"Go cruel, go! go with such peace, such rest,
  Such joy, such comfort as thou leav'st me here;
My angry soul, discharg'd from this weak breast,
  Shall haunt thee ever and attend thee near,
And fury-like, in snakes and firebrands dress'd,
  Shall aye torment thee whom it late held dear.
And if thou scape the seas, the rocks, and sands,
And come to fight amid the pagan bands,

There lying wounded 'mongst the hurt and slain,
  Of these my wrongs thou shalt the vengeance bear,
And oft Armida shalt thou call in vain
  At thy last gasp; this hope I soon to hear."
Here fainted she, with sorrow, grief, and pain,
  Her latest words scarce well expressèd were,
But in a swoon on earth outstretched she lies,
Stiff were her frozen limbs, clos'd were her eyes.

Wak'd from her trance, forsaken, speechless, sad,
  Armida wildly stared and gazed about;
"And is he gone," quoth she, "nor pity had
  To leave me thus 'twixt life and death in doubt?
Could he not stay? could not the traitor lad
  From this last trance help or recall me out?
And do I love him still, and on this sand
Still unreveng'd, still mourn, still weeping stand?"

translated by Edward Fayrfax: *Godfrey of
Bulloigne, or the Recoverie of Jerusalem* (1600)

44

5. SFOGAVA CON LE STELLE

Source: Madrigals, Book IV, 1603 (Venice, Ricciardo Amadino)

This is the first known setting by Monteverdi of a poem by his Florentine friend Ottavio Rinuccini, later described by Sir John Hawkins as 'a man of wit, handsome in person, polite, eloquent, and a very good poet'. Perhaps Monteverdi had heard Caccini sing his expressive version for solo tenor, eventually published in *Le Nuove Musiche* of 1602, for the style he uses in this polyphonic setting clearly aims at an audible projection of the text by means of *falso bordone* sections. This kind of musical declamation, so much like natural speech-rhythm, had been strongly recommended for certain types of music by Angelo Ingegneri in a treatise dated 1598 and published at Ferrara, where Monteverdi had (according to his dedication) received many honours and favours from the members of the Accademia degli Intrepidi.

Performance: The *falso bordone* sections are here fleshed out by definite rhythms in order to give singers an idea of the flow required. These passages, often unduly hurried in performance, should be sung in a steady and deliberate manner. Bars 27-30: ensure that the pronunciation is 'la sua', not 'la swa'. Again (39-53) the declamation must be calm, prayerful, but not hurried. Tune the dissonances most carefully throughout the coda.

Sfogava con le stelle	Together with the stars
Un infermo d'amore	A man sick with love
Sotto notturno ciel il suo dolore,	Poured out his sorrow beneath a night sky,
E dicea, fisso in loro:	And said, gazing upon them:
"O immagini belle	"O lovely images
De l'idol mio ch'adoro,	Of the idol whom I adore,
Si come a me mostrate	Just as you show me,
Mentre così splendete	While thus you shine,
La sua rara beltate,	Her rare beauty;
Così mostraste a lei	So show to her,
Mentre cotanto ardete,	While so much you burn,
I vivi ardori miei.	My own feelings of passion.
La fareste, col vostr' aureo sembiante,	Make her, with your golden likeness,
Pietosa, sì, come me fate amante".	Merciful indeed, as you make me a lover".
Ottavio Rinuccini	translated by D. S.

[N.B.: 'infermo' in line 2 is correct in 1603; later editions give the faulty reading 'inferno'. Compare the phrase 'ond'io, che sono inferma d'amore sotto questo notturno cielo', in G. B. Andreini's play *La Turca*, Act 1, Scene 1.]

52

6. LUCI SERENE E CHIARE

Source: Madrigals, Book IV, 1603 (Venice, Ricciardo Amadino)

Ridolfo Arlotti, a Ferrarese musician and poet who could sing well at sight (tenor or falsetto) and was praised for his light lyrics as 'a man accustomed to writing good things in this genre', belonged to the privileged circle of Count Alfonso Fontanelli and Carlo Gesualdo, Prince of Venosa. The first madrigal of Gesualdo's Fourth Book (1596) is a setting of Arlotti's poem; and in view of Monteverdi's visits to Ferrara, his desire to dedicate some of his music to Alfonso II d'Este, and his eventual dedication of his anthology of 1603 to the Accademia degli Intrepidi (Alfonso having died in 1597), it is very likely that he met Gesualdo and his friends. But his setting of 'Luci serene e chiare' is quite different from that of Gesualdo: instead of repeating the opening music for lines 4-6 of the poem, as Gesualdo does, Monteverdi floats everything up a tone to E major, and the 'fire and blood' finale is much more exciting. The use of five pairs of semibreves at the very beginning of the madrigal ranks as 'eye-music' in the truest sense of the expression.

Performance: A highly effective method of contrasting the cool gaze of the beloved's eyes and their ability to inflame desire is to sing the opening four bars *non vibrato*, and the next seven with pronounced passion. A slight accent on each syllable of 'si strugg' e non si duol' helps to maintain the tension, while the more rapidly moving duets demand absolutely crisp clarity of enunciation. A deathly slow and quiet ending will help to draw out the musical agony of the final 'more e non langue'.

Luci serene e chiare,
Voi m'incendete, voi; ma prov' il core
Nell' incendio diletto, non dolore.
Dolci parole e care,
Voi mi ferite, voi; ma prov' il petto
Non dolor ne la piaga, ma diletto.
O miracol d'amore!
Alma ch'è tutta foco e tutta sangue,
Si strugge e non si duol, mor' e non langue.

Ridolfo Arlotti

Eyes serene and clear,
You inflame me, but let the heart
Find pleasure, not sorrow, in the fire.
Words sweet and dear,
You wound me, but let my breast
Find pleasure, not sorrow, in the ⌊wound.
O miracle of love!
The soul that is all fire and blood,
Is destroyed yet grieves not, dies ⌊yet does not languish.

translated by D. S.

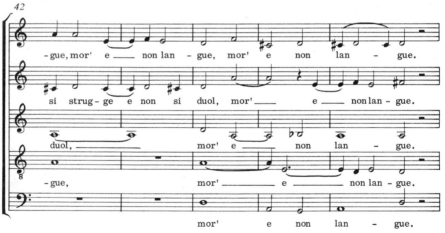

7. QUELL' AUGELLIN CHE CANTA

Source: Madrigals, Book IV, 1603 (Venice, Ricciardo Amadino)

The fast-growing popularity of Giambattista Guarini's tragi-comedy *Il Pastor Fido*, performed at Ferrara in 1595 and at Mantua in 1598, is reflected in the three excerpts set by Monteverdi and included in Book IV; and more was to come in Book V. Some of these settings could have been used in actual productions, music taking over from speech at various critical or strongly emotional points in the play. But the present madrigal follows Guarini's published text only in lines 1-7 and 9; lines 8, 10, and 11 either belong to an earlier unpublished version or were freely added. Alterations of comparable kind may be seen in several of Monteverdi's *Pastor Fido* compositions ('O primavera'; 'Anima mia, perdona'; 'Ch'io t'ami'), while those of Marenzio often remain faithful to the *editio princeps* of the play, as in his 1595 setting of 'Quell'augellin' (Book VII à 5). Both Marenzio and Monteverdi begin with a musical *riverenza* to the famous singing ladies of Ferrara, and there is a significant return to the trio of high voices in the present setting, from bars 37 to 45.

Performance: Monteverdi's avian melismata call not for speed but for gracefulness and lightness, and the distinction between direct and indirect speech can perhaps best be emphasized by means of dynamic level rather than any noticeable change of tempo. Nevertheless, a slight relaxation of pace may help the new thought from bars 25 to 30, after which the movement should remain constant.

Quell'augellin, che canta	That sweet little bird which sings
Sì dolcemente e lascivetto vola	So sweetly and flies so wantonly
Or da l'abete al faggio	Now from fir to beech
Et or dal faggio al mirto,	And now from beech to myrtle,
S'avesse umano spirto,	If it had a human soul
Direbb': "Ardo d'amore, ardo d'amore".	Would say, "I burn with love, I burn
Ma ben arde nel core	Its heart is full of love indeed⌐with love".
E chiam' il suo desio	And it calls to its mate
Che gli rispond': "Ardo d'amor' anch' io!"	Who replies to him:"I too burn with
Che sii tu benedetto,	Wherefore be thou blessed, ⌊love!"
Amoroso, gentil, vago augelletto.	Amorous, gentle, fair little bird!

Giambattista Guarini: *Il Pastor Fido*
(Act I, Scene 1; Linco to Silvio)

translated by D. S.

8. CH'IO T'AMI

Source: Madrigals, Book V, 1605 (Venice, Ricciardo Amadino)

The poetry of Guarini dominates Book V, just as that of Tasso dominated Book II published fif-
teen years previously, and of the five extracts from *Il Pastor Fido* 'Ecce Silvio' is in five sections
and 'Ch'io t'ami' in three. This latter group is here presented as an uninterrupted whole, even
though Monteverdi omits 28 lines at the end of the first section (bar 39). Three more lines are
omitted after 'che sì rigida ninfa' in the final section, the effect being to tighten up the syntax
by removing a purely parenthetical statement. These changes may have been dictated by the
circumstances of a stage production, where from time immemorial texts have been freely tam-
pered with in the interests of dramaturgy. The fact that this excerpt contains the essence of
Mirtillo's declaration of love for Amarilli explains why the tenor part is so important: it leads
off at the beginning of the first and third sections, and occasionally comes forward as soloist,
as in bars 117 to 122. Yet elsewhere it lacks essential lines which appear only in the other parts,
and in view of this it seems highly unlikely that the scene was performed as a tenor solo accompanied by instruments, as has occasionally been surmised.

Performance: The predominance of homophonic texture lends the music an air of ease in performance, but this can prove to be a deception. Any attempt to heighten the emotional pitch of a
word or phrase by means of subtle shifts of tempo depends, for its success, on the precision
and cohesion of the ensemble. The singers must breathe, phrase, think, and move together. The
projection of speech rhythm and accent is of prime importance: a slight pause often helps to
emphasize a key word, as for instance the imperative 'mori' in bars 106 and 116. Flexibility
dependent on the emotional content of both music and poetry will best bring the work to life.

Ch'io t'ami, e t'ami più de la mia vita,	That I love you, yes, love you more than my life —
Se tu no'l sai, crudele,	If you do not know this, cruel one,
Chiedilo a queste selve	Ask it of these woods
Che te 'l diranno, e te 'l diran con esse	And they will tell you; so too
Le fere lor' e i duri sterpi e i sassi	Will their wild beasts, and the rough thickets and ⌊the rocks
Di questi alpestri monti,	Of those high mountains,
Ch' i' ho sì spesse volte	Which so many times
Inteneriti al suon de' miei lamenti.	I have softened with the sound of my lamenting.
Deh! bella e cara e sì soave un tempo,	Alas! lovely, precious, and once so gentle
Cagion del viver mio, mentre al ciel ⌊piacque,	Motive for my living — while it pleased heaven —
Volgi una volta, e volgi	Turn now, yes, turn on me
Quelle stelle amorose,	Those fond eyes
Come le vidi mai, così tranquille	As I once saw them, so calm
E piene di pietà, prima ch' io moia,	And full of kindness, before I die,
Chè 'l morir mi sia dolce.	So that death may be sweet.
E dritto è ben che se mi furo un tempo	It is right and proper that if they were once
Dolci segni di vita, or sien di morte	Sweet tokens of life, now deathly
Quei begl' occhi amorosi	Are those lovely eyes
E quel soave sguardo.	And that soft glance.
Chi mi scorse ad amare	She who led me on to love
Mi scorg' anco a morire,	Let her also guide me to my death,
E chi fu l'alba mia	And she who was my dawn
Del mio cadente dì, l'Espero or sia.	Let her be the evening-star of my darkening day.
Ma tu, più che mai dura,	But you, more than ever unkind,
Favilla di pietà non senti ancora;	Still feel no spark of pity!
Anzi t'inaspri più, quanto più prego.	Rather do you grow more harsh, the more I ⌊entreat you.
Così senza parlar dunque m'ascolti?	Do you hear me then, in silence?
A chi parlo infelice a un muto sasso?	To whom do I speak, wretch that I am, to a mute ⌊rock?
S'altro non mi vuoi dir, dimmi almen ⌊"mori!"	If you can say no more, at least bid me die;
E morir mi vedrai.	And you shall see me die.
Quest' è ben, empi' Amor, miseria ⌊estrema,	This is indeed, O wicked Love, the depths of ⌊misery,
Che sì rigida ninfa	That the heartless nymph
Non mi risponda, e l'armi	Answers me not, and the weapon
D'una sola sdegnosa e cruda voce	Of a single harsh and disdainful word
Sdegni di proferire	She refuses to offer me
Al mio morir.	At my death.

Giambattista Guarini: *Il Pastor Fido*
(Act III, Scene 3; Mirtillo to Amarilli)

translated by D. S.

9. ZEFIRO TORNA

Source: Madrigals, Book VI, 1614 (Venice, Ricciardo Amadino)

Alone among Monteverdi's madrigal collections, Book VI has no apparent dedicatee. This was due not to a deliberate oversight, but to a change in the composer's life-style brought about by his move from Mantua to Venice. He had no patron to whom the book could be dedicated, and what was more important its contents reflected so much of his former triumphs and sorrows that he probably preferred it to appear under no aegis but his own. The book falls into two balanced sections, each comprising a Lament, a sonnet by Petrarch, and a group of continuo madrigals. A seven-part dialogue brings the collection to a noble close. The two Petrarch sonnets, both taken from the latter part of the *Rime* ('After Laura's Death'), almost certainly date from the summer of 1607, when the composer sent two new settings of sonnets for unaccompanied voices to Sampierdarena, near Genoa, where Duke Vincenzo was on vacation.

Performance: The notation of sections in triple time has been halved in order to clarify the metrical relationship between bars 9-11 and 45-47. Clearly the two bass notes leading into bar 10, and the corresponding tenor notes ('e'l bel') leading into bar 11 should agree in tempo. Philomel's lamenting calls for a slight ritenuto, just as Jove's rejoicing needs an empyreal fullness of tone. Sustain the dissonances and pursue an inexorable increase of tension throughout the last eighteen bars.

Zefiro torna e 'l bel tempo rimena	Zephyrus brings the time that sweetly scenteth,
E i fiori e l'erbe, sua dolce famiglia,	With flowers and herbs, and winter's frost exileth,
E garrir Progne e pianger Filomena,	Progne now chirpeth, and Philomel lamenteth,
E primavera candida e vermiglia;	Flora the garlands white and red compileth,
Ridono i prati, e 'l ciel si rasserena;	Fields do rejoice, the frowning sky relenteth,
Giove s'allegra di mirar sua figlia;	Jove to behold his dearest daughter smileth,
L'aria e l'acqua e la terra è d'amor piena,	Th'air, the water, the earth to Joy consenteth,
Ogni animal d'amar si riconsiglia.	Each creature now to love, him reconcileth.
Ma per me, lasso, tornano i più gravi	But with me, wretch, the storms of woe persever,
Sospiri, che del cor profondo tragge	And heavy sighs, which from my heart she straineth,
Quella ch' al ciel se ne portò le chiavi,	That took the key thereof to heaven for ever.
E cantar augelletti, e fiorir piagge,	So that singing of birds and springtime flowering,
E'n belle donne onesti atti e soavi	And ladies' love that men's affection gaineth,
Sono un deserto, e fere aspre e selvagge.	Are like a desert, and cruel beasts devouring.

Petrarch: Sonnet CCCX

N. Yonge: *Musica Transalpina* (London, 1588)

10. OIMÈ IL BEL VISO

Source: Madrigals, Book VI, 1614 (Venice, Ricciardo Amadino)

Since many of its texts deal with death, lamentation, parting, unrequited love, Monteverdi may have thought of Book VI as a musical memorial to his wife Claudia, who died in 1607, and to Caterina Martinelli, the gifted young singer intended for the title role of *Arianna*, who died of smallpox in 1608. Certainly the intense feeling with which he imbued Petrarch's lament for Laura betrays a strong personal involvement that is lacking in his earlier madrigals. His friend Abbot Angelo Grillo noticed it at once, and wrote to G. B. Magnavacca: '... in these last madrigals especially, his melancholy and forceful eloquence appeals to the most jaded ears. To be sure, the music has so much new in it that trained voices and assurance are essential to perform it'.

Performance: The individual phrases of the solemn opening should be quietly arched so that the sighs above can be heard without forcing of tone. Aim for a clearly focussed sound at 'Il dolce riso', while the upper voices bring out their dissonances with relentless persistence. 'Alma real' requires a total change of mood and sound, at once gentler and yet noble. The many subsequent variations of texture, with different trios and quartets, call for skilful tonal balance.

Oimè il bel viso, oimè il soave sguardo,	Alas, the fair countenance, Alas, the gentle glance!
Oimè il leggiadro portamento altero!	Alas, the proud and graceful bearing!
Oimè il parlar ch' ogn' aspr' ingegn' e fero	Alas, the speech, for thou didst humble
Faceva umìle ed ogni uom vil gagliardo!	Every harsh nature, and lend spirit to the cowardly!
Et oimè il dolce riso ond' uscì il dardo	And alas, the sweet laughter whence came the dart
Di che morte, altro ben gia mai non spero!	From which I crave no other boon than death!
Alma real, dignissima d'impero	Queenly soul, most worthy of empire,
Se non fosse fra noi scesa sì tardo!	If only thou hadst not come down to us so tardily.
Per voi convien ch'io arda, e'n voi respire,	For all you, her attributes, I must burn, and in you breathe,
Ch'i' pur fui vostro, e se di voi son privo	Since I too was yours; and if deprived of you
Via men d' ogni sventura altra mi dole.	I suffer as from no other ill.
Di speranza m'empieste e di desire	You filled me with hope and with desire,
Quand' io partì dal sommo piacer vivo:	When I departed from the greatest joy of my life:
Ma'l vento ne portava le parole.	But the wind carried our words away.

Petrarch: Sonnet CCLXVII   translated by D. S.

Printed in England by West Central Printing Co. Ltd., London and Suffolk